Nottingham C

on old picture p(

Grenville Jennings

COPYRIGHT NHM.2 L.L.   KING ST. & QUEEN ST. NOTTINGHAM.   PEVERIL SERIES. 6005

1. A 'Peveril' series postcard showing a scene looking up to the junction of King and Queen Streets from Long Row. A lone constable stands on point duty surrounded by a sea of cobblestones. The card was sent to Bournemouth in August 1922.

£3.50

Introduction

When the Post Office relented its rule in 1902 that allowed messages to be written on the reverse of postcards, the floodgates of postcard collecting opened dramatically, and within a very short time millions of cards were being produced on every conceivable subject.

Quite naturally, as today, the public liked their relatives and friends to see views of the town, or places where they were taking holidays, so many of the topographical cards published were of local tourist attractions, town centres, parks, churches and the like - Nottingham being no exception to this.

There are so many views of the Market Place, the Castle, Arboretum or Trent Bridge to make even the earliest Edwardian scenes very common. For collectors today, it is the views of the back streets of towns that are most elusive, as many of the top postcard publishers of the day mainly ignored them. W.H. Smith and C. & A.G. Lewis (a local publisher) produced many fine photographic cards of the city, as did the other local publisher, Albert Hindley, in his 'Clumber' series, which was similar to the cards of an unknown publisher of the 'Peveril' series.

Back street scenes themselves may appear relatively dull, apart from where the photographer has cajoled local children to provide animation, but we must remember that in the early 1900's motorised transport was almost non-existent, and leisure time at a premium.

The cards shown are a mixture of views reflecting our city in the early years of the last century, and bring back memories of places sadly no longer with us.

Grenville Jennings
June 2001

Front cover: an early morning view outside the Old Exchange, Market Place, Nottingham c. 1907. The Thorneycroft bus shown was one of the fleet withdrawn in June 1908 due to expense and unrealiability. This postcard, sent to Coventry in September 1907, was published by Albert Hindley in his 'Clumber' series, named after the street where his premises were.

Back cover (top): Narrow Marsh. If ever a card portrayed life in early Edwardian Nottingham, then this one in the 'Clumber' series is it! To the left is the "Star and Garter" lodging house; many of the other properties in Narrow Marsh were of a similar nature.

(bottom): the photo on this 'Peveril' series card of the Walter Fountain is taken from Greyfriars Gate. On the building to the left, at the corner of Lister Gate and Broad Marsh, is a sign, 'Broad Marsh,' which can still be seen today adjacent to the Lister Gate entrance to the shopping centre.

No 473   THE EXCHANGE, NOTTINGHAM MARKET.

2. A 'Clumber' series photographic card of the Exchange Building with market stalls filling the Market Square - an idyllic scene just prior to the outbreak of World War One. Little did the people strolling around here in the sunshine realise the horrors to come.

3. A close-up of the old Exchange Building on a c. 1920 photographic card published by A. Spree showing some of the shops on the ground floor.

4. A crowded Market Place with a carrier and his horse-drawn cart on a card published by Charles Voisey of London. It was posted to Maidstone in August 1905.

POULTRY.

NOTTINGHAM.

2907

5. Looking up the Poultry, with a Crouch's parcel van to the right, and to the left a well-laden early pram. The card was sent to Harby, Lincoln, in October 1905.

6. Long Row, showing the famous "Black Boy Hotel" c. 1907. How on earth city planners agreed for this building to be replaced by a modern store remains a mystery to many of Nottingham's citizens to this day. 'Clumber' series postcard no. 139, sent to Peebles in 1909.

7. A busy Long Row looking towards the Market Place on a card published by C. & A.G. Lewis which was sent to a serving soldier with the British Expeditionary Force in France in December 1916. It is most interesting to note that apart from a distant tram, all other transport is horse-drawn.

THE NEW EXCHANGE, NOTTINGHAM.   No. 3621.

This magnificent building was commenced in May, 1926, and is expected to be completed in February. 1929, at a approx. cost of £500,000. The material required for its construction includes 4,000 scaffolding poles. 3.500 putlogs for scaffold floors, and 72,000 yds. of wire rope. The building has a frontage of 120 ft., and stands 200 ft. high, covering an area of 40,000 sq. ft. The ventilating shaft seen in the dome measures 7 ft. 6 ins. in diameter

8. Almost there! The new Council House, begun in 1926, nears completion for 1929, though the shops of the Old Exchange can still be seen. C & A.G. Lewis card no. 3621. Architect on the project was T. Cecil Howitt.

NEW EXCHANGE BUILDINGS NOTTINGHAM

T. Cecil Howitt
A.R.I.B.A.
Architect.

REX SERIES
311.

9. 'Rex' series postcard showing the completed magnificent Council House.

Market Place, Nottingham.

10. An informal 'Pot Market' on the cobbles of the Market Square near Queen Victoria's monument. Publisher of the card was T. Leak of Carrington Street.

130 IN MARKET SQUARE, NOTTINGHAM.

11. Horse-drawn transport vies with the no. 12 tram at the side of the 'Pot Market' situated between Angel and Long Rows. W.H. Smith 'Central' series card no. 130.

12. As today, the busiest part of Long Row between Market Street and Queen Street had an abundance of shops, though D. Flack and Co. advertising costumes, mantles and furs would not be very popular in certain circles. 'Rex' series card no. 119 from the early 1920's.

13. Views of the Market Place are relatively common, though this one, taken from Griffin & Spalding's first floor shop window, is not. We see in the background the Pot Market and the premises along Beastmarket Hill and Angel Row. Card published by W.H. Smith and sent in May 1913.

14. Even though Clumber Street was open to motorised traffic in the 1920's, we have a typical scene of the times where pedestrians were more prominent than transport. C. & A.G. Lewis card no. 3300.

15. In August 1908 Ashton's Yard, Bridlesmith Gate, was reported by the *Nottingham Daily Express* to have recently been one of the grimiest little slums in Nottingham - but now was transformed!

16. Bridlesmith Gate on a 'Rex' series postcard, no. 171. The lady to the left of the card is looking into the window of John Dann, confectioner, at no. 21.

17. Lister Gate on a 'City and Wollaton' series card no. 9 published about 1905.

18. A horse and dray wend their way up Wheeler Gate, with St. Peter's Church in the background.

19. Lister Gate looking down towards the Walter Fountain and Carrington Street c. 1914. 'Peveril' series card no. 3046.

20. An attractive card of the Walter Fountain at the bottom of Lister Gate and adjacent to Broad Marsh to the right. The card, from London publishers A. & G. Taylor, was sent to Farnborough, Hampshire in August 1908. The fountain was removed in 1950 for road widening.

21. It is hard to imagine that the Broad Marsh Centre now occupies the view of Carrington Street seen on this C. & A.G. Lewis card no. 152 from around 1922.

22. Locally published by W. Coppock, 210 Arkwright Street, this postcard shows a view of Carrington Street looking towards the Midland Station.

550 P   NEW BUILDINGS. CARRINGTON STREET. NOTTINGHAM.

23. The junction of Canal Street and Carrington Street c. 1912 on a 'Clumber' series photographic card from Albert Hindley. G. Hardy & Company's shop is on the right, and the entrance to the current Broad Marsh Bus Terminal to the right of that. Postcards of this area of the city are relatively scarce.

24. Another view of the Canal Street/Carrington Street junction, this time on C. & A.G. Lewis card no. 150. It was sent by Auntie P. to Doris in Bristol in July 1922.

25. Cullen Bros. was a very well-known and respected store located on the station side of Canal Street and Carrington Street. 'Peveril' series postcard no. 3049.

26. Carrington Street, probably in the late 1920's, outside the "Gresham Hotel." Pedestrians stream along, on their way to and from the station or Arkwright Street.

27. Station Street showing Boots the Chemists' head office and on the left, on the corner of Trent Street, the "Wellington" public house. Another C. & A.G. Lewis postcard.

28. The corner of Spaniel Row and Friar Lane seen on a privately-published card.

29. The Theosophical Hall, Friar Lane, Nottingham, which was the meeting place of the Friends Society, the Quakers.

30. A fine artistic view of Friar Lane by Charles Flower in a series of postcards (*"Oilette"* no. 1783 - Nottingham) published by Raphael Tuck early last century. It was posted to Nantwich in August 1904.

31. The "Hearty Goodfellow" public house was located at no. 43 Mount Street. Peter Gavin was the landlord in the 1920's.

MILTON STREET, NOTTINGHAM

32. A fine view of Milton Street, Nottingham. In the background is the "Corner Pin" public house, sadly no longer with us. A 'Peveril' real photo series postcard.

MIDLAND STATION AND CARRINGTON STREET, NOTTINGHAM

33. A busy scene outside the Midland Station, completed in January 1904. A 'Castle' series card published by J.P.B., Nottingham.

34. Posted on 14th September 1931 to Torquay, this card (published by Spree) c
Upper Parliament Street shows to the left the premises of the Nottingham furnishin
company, owned by Sir Julien Cahn, the Nottinghamshire cricketing benefactor.

Parliment St. Nott.

35. A relatively scarce view by an anonymous publisher of the interior of the Midland Station about 1905.

Victoria Station & Hotel, Nottingham.

36. Opened in 1900, all that remains of the magnificent Victoria Station, now replaced by the shopping centre, is the clock tower and recently renovated Victoria Hotel. A 'Clumber' series postcard.

GREAT CENTRAL : LONDON EXPRESS AT NOTTINGHAM.   A.J.MILNE

37. Another scarce interior station view, this time of Victoria, featuring a London-bound Great Central train. Photo by A.J. Milne.

38. A 'birds eye' view taken from the top of the Victoria Hotel of Mansfield Road. To the right, the large prominent building is the Nottingham Brewery Ltd. In the far distance can be seen St. Andrew's church. A 'City and Wollaton' series card, posted to Southend in December 1908.

39. Burton Street, Nottingham, showing, to the right, the Guildhall, and to the left the "Guildhall Inn." 'Peveril' series no. 3061.

THE BLUECOAT SCHOOL, NOTTINGHAM.

40. Founded in 1706, the Bluecoat School was originally on the corner of Mansfield Road and Bluecoat Street.

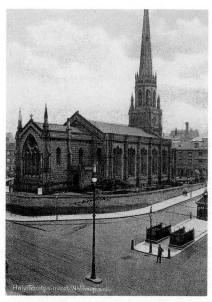

41. Holy Trinity Church, Trinity Square, now the site of a municipal car park. *"Am sending to help with your album,"* wrote Lizzie to Hilda Salmon at Great Yarmouth in October 1908.

505   Mansfield Rd.   Nottingham

42. Taken from outside the Bluecoat School, this postcard looks down Mansfield Road, with Woodborough Road and the Wesleyan Chapel to the left.

Mansfield Road, Nottingham.

43. A relatively uncommon view of Mansfield Road c. 1913, showing the properties on the right hand side between Woodborough and Union Roads. Prominent is the Nottingham Brewery at nos 52-56.

197 WAVERLEY STREET, NOTTINGHAM.

44. A fine study of Waverley Street about 1910 at the junction of Peel and Clarendon Streets with Shakespeare Street on a W.H. Smith postcard, no. 197.

Goldsmith St.

45. Goldsmith Street looking towards Waverley Street and the Arboretum. To the right, at the corner of Shakespeare Street, can be seen the Post Office. Card published by Spree and posted to a London address in March 1910.

46. In the distance, looking down Oxford Street, can be seen the new Albert Hall. This was dedicated in 1908, replacing the old one destroyed by fire in 1906. 'Rex' series card no. 153, sent to a Warwickshire address in November 1927.

47. Another elusive back street view, this time of Dryden Street at the junction with Shakespeare Street. The card was posted to Stamford in December 1909.

48. Dryden Street close to the junction with Peel Street. In the foreground of the card are piles of horse manure spread across the cobbles, a common street problem in pre-1914 Nottingham.

ADDISON STREET, NOTTINGHAM

49. Compared to the other cards, this view of Addison Street on a W.H. Smith series postcard is crowded! But, once again, no transport in sight.

50. A leafy Gill Street on a Spree postcard of about 1910. Someone has written on the back of the card: *"This is one of the finest streets in Notts."*

292   SHAKESPEARE STREET, NOTTINGHAM.

51. Plenty of youthful volunteers pose for the photographer on W.H. Smith postcard no. 292 of Shakespeare Street.

52. The Guildhall decorations for the coronation of 1911 on a postcard published by H.E. Marshall.

53. The "Clarendon Hotel" changed its name in 1913 to the "Rufford" and then to the "County Hotel" in August 1923. The site now forms part of the Concert Hall complex. This advertising card was posted to Bexhill in October 1905.

54. Looking down into Theatre Square from Wollaton Street. The "Royal Hippodrome" on the left is long gone, but the shop facades on the left are similar today. This card was posted to Sheffield in August 1920.

55. A superb photographic postcard of Theatre Square in the 'Peveril' series - note the absence of traffic apart from the brewer's dray delivery cart, presumably supplying the Theatre Royal.

56. A splendid array of horse-drawn transport waits outside the Theatre Royal c. 1910. To the right is the statue of Samuel Morley. Another 'Peveril' series postcard.

57. The Theatre Royal and, down the right hand side, the famous Empire Theatre of Varieties on South Sherwood Street. This opened in February 1898, sadly closing in June 1958. This card came from London publishers Hartmann, and was sent to Norwich in September 1913.

58. Chapel Bar looking towards Derby Road on a 'Peveril' series postcard no. 561, c. 1912.

59. The writer of this card tells the 'Misses Marshall' of Woolston, Southampton, *"Our side of Park Row, showing 21 where we reside (sleep at any rate) also 29 where I stayed."*

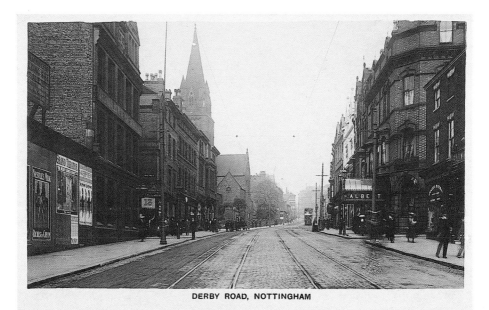

DERBY ROAD, NOTTINGHAM

60. Derby Road, with the "Albert Hotel" to the right. At this time the road carried traffic in both directions. A Boots the Chemists postcard published c. 1910.

61. The People's College private board school c. 1904, situated at 11 College Street behind St. Barnabas Cathedral. At this time it was known as the public elementary school and was for boys only; previously as People's College it was for both boys and girls. A 'Peveril' series card, posted from Beeston to Birmingham in October 1905.

REGENT STREET, NOTTINGHAM

62. Regent Street in 1912 was, as today, used mainly by the medical profession, being so close to the general hospital. A 'Peveril' real photo series card, sent to Gloucester in September 1912.

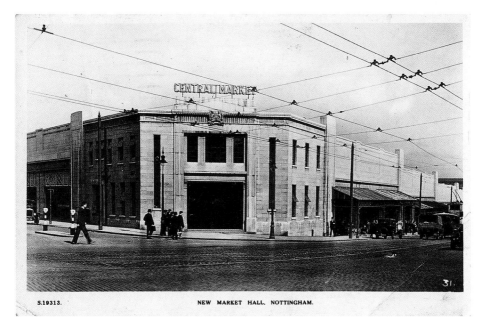

S.19313.   NEW MARKET HALL, NOTTINGHAM.

63. This W.H. Smith 1920's postcard view of the New Market Hall (central market) shows the entrance from Glasshouse and King Edward Streets. The market is now in the Victoria Centre complex.

The-Palais-de-Danse, Nottingham. No. 3297.

64. A most familiar city centre landmark was the Nottingham Palais de Danse. The writer of this C. & A.G. Lewis card, sent to France, advises *"C'est un beau Palais."* It was actually built on the site of the old borough prison.

65. A postcard published by Blakey Bros. of Nottingham featuring Stoney Street in the Lace Market. *"1 o'clock girls going to dinner"* wrote Alice to Amy.

LEAVING THE LACE MARKET, NOTTINGHAM.

66. Taken from Broad Street at the junction with Carlton Street, this 1911 postcard once again illustrates lace workers. ' Peveril' series no. 220.